LENTEN REFLECTIONS FROM

A FATHER WHO KEEPS HIS PROMISES

LENTEN REFLECTIONS FROM A FATHER WHO KEEPS HIS PROMISES

Scott Hahn

SERVANT BOOKS

PUBLISHED BY FRANCISCAN MEDIA
Cincinnati, Ohio

Daily reflections excerpted from *A Father Who Keeps His Promises: God's Covenant Love in Scripture* by Scott Hahn, © 1998 Scott Hahn, Ph.D. All rights reserved. Used by permission.

Cover design by Candle Light Studios
Cover image: Christ's Charge to Peter, c.1616 (oil on oak panel) by Rubens, Peter Paul (1577-1640); 139.2x114.8 cm;
© Wallace Collection, London, UK | bridgemanart.com
Book design by Mark Sullivan

ISBN 978-1-61636-497-7
Copyright © 2012 Scott Hahn, Ph.D. All rights reserved.

Published by Servant Books, an imprint of Franciscan Media.
28 W. Liberty St.
Cincinnati, OH 45202

Printed in the United States of America.
Printed on acid-free paper.
12 13 14 15 16 5 4 3 2 1

Contents

Introduction

I can't think of anything more worth sharing during Lent than the biblical story of God's covenant love in salvation history. Each day, beginning with Ash Wednesday and ending with Divine Mercy Sunday, this book provides a different reflection for each day, providing as a whole a simple retelling of the stories that make up *the* Story.

For the most part, I stick to the major characters and events, since these stories make up the Bible's main plot. My primary goal is to provide the "big picture," which has been lost to many readers of Scripture in our day. In the process, I also hope to show how much practical wisdom the Bible contains for the ordinary believer, especially "rank and file" Catholics. This is one of the reasons I emphasize the twin themes of covenant and family, because they touch us right where we live. The other reason for focusing on these closely related themes is that the Bible itself does.

Lent bids us to return to the innocence of baptism. As Noah and his family were saved through the waters of the deluge, we were saved through the waters of baptism. God's covenant with Noah marked the start of a new world, but it also prefigured a new and greater covenant between God and his creation.

Jesus is portrayed as the new Adam—the beloved son of God, living in harmony with the wild beasts, and being served by angels. Like Adam, he too is tempted by the devil. But while Adam fell, giving reign to sin and death, Jesus is victorious. This is the good news, the "gospel of God" that Christ proclaims. Through his death, resurrection, and enthronement at the right hand of the Father, the world is once again made God's kingdom.

In the waters of baptism, each of us entered the kingdom of God's beloved Son. We were made children of God, new creations. But like Jesus, and Israel before him, we have passed through the baptismal waters only to be driven into the wilderness—a world filled with afflictions and tests of our faithfulness. We are led on this journey by Jesus, our Savior; he feeds us with the bread of angels and cleanses our consciences in the sacrament of reconciliation.

So, as you begin your Lenten journey, prepare to reflect on the greatest story of all and the Father who keeps his promises.

Lent Begins

| GOD'S MASTER PLAN |

Scripture testifies to how God has cared for his family throughout the ages, making a way for his children to live with him forever. The biblical record shows that our heavenly Father has kept each and every one of his promises he swore concerning our redemption at the cost of his only beloved Son. Because of God's grace, the gift of salvation is free, but it is not cheap.

We'll look at the story of that unfailing love this Lenten season. We'll examine together what God has done in history to make us his family and to save us from the wretched misery of our own sin and selfishness. We'll discover anew how passionately he seeks us, how firm is his intention to make us whole again, and how deserving he is to receive our gratitude, trust, and obedience.

This Lent, my hope is that you will catch a new vision of the eternal Father who never fails to fulfill his word. No matter what obstacles arise, he never loses sight of his goal: to form and fashion a human family to share in the infinite love of the Trinity. As you consider how God has fathered his people over the ages, hopefully you will realize more fully how great God's love is for you as a member of his covenant family.

ASH WEDNESDAY

God's Unfailing Love

"See what love the Father has given us,
that we should be called children of God."

—1 John 3:1

We constantly hear about fathers who become so engrossed in pursuing a career or some other goal that they end up seriously neglecting their children. The trite phrase "quality time" often describes their efforts to make the most of the little time they do give. Even the best of fathers are all too human, flawed creatures who sometimes break their promises or fail to be around when their children need them most.

I know that's true of my own efforts at fathering. Despite my best intentions to follow through on family commitments, inevitably some other pressing concern arises to wreck the plans we've made together and take me away from home. Even though I try very hard not to make explicit promises I might not be able to keep, still my kids are disappointed when the expectations that I encouraged are dashed by unexpected circumstances—some of my own making.

I want to help you catch a vision of a very different kind of father, the eternal Father who never fails to fulfill his word. No matter what obstacles arise, he never loses sight of his goal: to form and fashion a human family to share in the infinite love of the Trinity. As we consider what Scripture tells us about how God has fathered his people over the ages, we should realize more fully just how great God's personal love for each and every one of us is, as members of his covenant family.

+ How has my earthly father shaped my understanding of God as Father? Do I believe that my heavenly Father loves me with an unfailing love?

Lord, help me to respond to your great love for me with true gratitude and trust. As Lent begins, I want to deepen my understanding of what it means to be part of your covenant family.

THURSDAY AFTER ASH WEDNESDAY

Divine Discipline

"We have had earthly fathers to discipline us and we
respected them. Shall we not much more be subject to
the Father of spirits and live? For they disciplined us for
a short time at their pleasure, but he disciplines us for
our good, that we may share his holiness."

—Hebrews 12:7–10

Our heavenly Father has been watching over us throughout all of
history, saving us from destruction over and over again. He longs
to convince us of his passionate love for each one of us, that relent-
less mercy which calls and enables us to share his own divine life,
that fiery outpouring of love by which the Father eternally begets
the Son in the Holy Spirit. Only an infinite, raging love such as
appears among the Blessed Trinity can explain the mysteries of
human sin and salvation.

Let's face it: we humans really don't want God to love us *that*
much. It's simply too demanding. Obedience is one thing, but
this sort of love clearly calls for more than keeping commandments. It calls for nothing less than self-donation. That might
not be a difficult job for the three infinite Persons of the Trinity,
but for creatures like us, such love is a summons to martyrdom.

This invitation requires much more suffering and self-denial than simply giving up chocolate for Lent. It demands nothing less than a constant dying to self.

+ What additional sacrifice can I make today to affirm my desire to be disciplined this Lent?

Lord, whatever I've decided to give up for Lent, let me use that small sacrifice to remind me of the continual self-denial you call me to. And most of all, let me remember the reason for your call to be able to participate in your divine life!

FRIDAY AFTER ASH WEDNESDAY

Temporal Loss—Eternal Gain

"He...partook of the same nature, that through death he
might destroy him who has the power of death, that is,
the devil, and deliver all those who through fear of death
were subject to lifelong bondage."
—Hebrews 2:14–15

Our stay on earth is only meant to be temporary. The New
Testament integrates the "otherworldly" orientation of the Old
Testament into God's fatherly plan to teach his children in
different stages to desire and obtain that which is divine and
eternal. As Jesus taught, the only way into heaven is to lovingly
divest ourselves of the temporal goods of earth (see Matthew 5–7).
This is not because earthly things are bad. On the contrary, it's
precisely because earthly things are so good second only to heavenly ones that we're able to sacrifice the former to gain the latter.

Sin is thus exposed for what it really is: our refusal to live
according to the perfect love of the Trinity. This divine love is
reflected in the sacrificial requirements of the laws of the covenant. At the same time, we are enabled to grasp the inner logic of
salvation, and to comprehend how it could only be accomplished
through Jesus's sacrificial death on the cross. For that is where

Christ took our humanity and transformed it into a perfect image and instrument of the Trinity's life-giving love, as a sacrificial gift of self.

+ Is there clutter in my life that I've been clinging to? What could I do to simplify my life and sharpen my eternal focus?

Heavenly Father, help me to see that earthly goods are nothing when compared to the eternal treasures you long to give us. Thank you for this earthly journey, meant to lead us all to our true home with you in heaven!

Contracts and Covenants

"I will live in them and move among them, and I will be
their God, and they shall be my people. Therefore come
out from them, and be separate from them, says the Lord,
and touch nothing unclean; then I will welcome you."
—2 Corinthians 6:16–18

What exactly is a covenant? It comes from the Latin word *convener,*
which means "to come together" or "to agree"; the English term
"covenant" involves a formal, solemn, and binding pact between
two or more parties. Each party must live up to its end of the
bargain. By this definition, a covenant is similar to a contract.
However, in biblical terms, covenants involve much more than
contracts.

For ancient Israelites, a covenant differed from a contract about
as much as marriage differed from prostitution. When a man and
woman marry, they declare their undying love for one another
until death, but a prostitute sells her body to the highest bidder
and then moves on to the next customer. So contracts make people
customers, employees, clients, whereas covenants turn them into
spouses, parents, children, siblings. In short, covenants are made
to forge bonds of sacred kinships.

So if you want to get to the heart of Scripture, think covenant not contract, father not judge, family room not courtroom; God's laws and judgments are meant to be interpreted as signs of his fatherly love, wisdom, and authority. The basic message God wants to convey by a covenant, then, can be stated simply: "I love you. I am committed to you. I swear that I will never forsake you. You are mine and I am yours. I am your father, and you are my family." How astonishing that God has such profound love for his creatures!

+ Do I treasure my brothers and sisters in the faith? What could I do today to express my love for a fellow believer?

Lord, the more I learn about how you've fathered your children down through the centuries, the more what you mean by a covenant becomes a reality for me, opening up new dimensions of your love. I am grateful to be a part of the household of faith.

Week One

| CREATION STORY |

Many readers of the Bible today are more interested in figuring out whether or not the Creation account in the book of Genesis can be squared with the theory of evolution than in discovering what the author really meant to say. Our modern preoccupation with science often gets in the way. In fact, the only time Scripture even raises the question *how* the world was created was in the book of Job, where God basically says to forget it (see Job 38–41). It's simply too hard for us even to imagine, much less figure out for ourselves.

Instead, the creation account seems to address some other—but no less important—questions, such as *what* and *why* God created. To see how these questions are addressed, Lent is a fitting time to reread Genesis through new eyes, as it were, by looking at it through old eyes. This means going back to the text in search of clues as to what the ancient writer intended to say to his original readers. A proper reading of Genesis calls for adhering to the narrative as closely as possible, reading it with great care and a critical empathy for the culture and time in which it was written and transmitted. If the creation account is approached and studied in this manner, the results will demonstrate a profound complementarity of religion and science, faith and reason.

From Chaos to Cosmos

"The earth was without form and void, and darkness
was upon the face of the deep; and the Spirit of God was
moving over the face of the waters."

—Genesis 1:2

The eternal love story of Scripture begins very simply: "In the beginning God created the heavens and the earth" (Genesis 1:1). Isn't it striking how easy it sounds? Without any exertion, or gods to fight off, God simply spoke, and...BOOM (or BANG, if you prefer): The entire universe—space, time, galaxies, solar systems, planets, molecules, subatomic particles—all of it burst into existence out of nothing. That's what I call power.

The Bible makes it clear from the outset that God is absolutely supreme, totally sovereign, all-powerful, and thus not to be confused in any way with the world he made. He alone is God, and we are not; nor is the vast cosmos his body or house (contrary to New Age teachings). "The heavens and the earth" point to the two main realms within creation: the spiritual and the material. The first one refers to the immaterial realm that is occupied by pure spirits, the "heavenly hosts" we call angels, while the second one points to the earthly habitat God made for humanity. Unlike the heavens, however, the earth was still in an incomplete state of *formlessness* and *emptiness*. The rest of the first chapter of Genesis narrates God's creative response to, and resolution of the earth's primordial chaotic condition. God transforms the earth—from chaos to cosmos—according to his power and plan.

> + What ways have I allowed myself to be influenced by the world's thinking? Where am I tempted to think I am self-sufficient, having no need of God?

Almighty God, I am in awe of your creation and your power. You alone are God; help me to always remember this.

The Sacredness of Human Life

"Then God said, 'Let us make man in our image, after
our likeness.... So God created man in his own image,
in the image of God he created him; male and female he
created them."
—Genesis 1:26–27

What does it really mean for us to be made, male and female,
in God's "image and likeness"? First, it means that human life
possesses great sacredness. Society often makes the mistake of
ascribing value according to a person's great works, good looks,
or economic productivity and output. This mistake was made by
the Nazis in World War II, and it is at the heart of the tragedy of
abortion and euthanasia in our time. The sanctity of human life
includes the preborn and aged, the physically infirm and mentally
impaired. Every person has this awesome and immeasurable
dignity because each human is made in God's image.

Second, it means that our work has special value. Society gets
it backwards. My labor isn't what confers dignity upon me; it is
bearing the image of God that invests my work with honor. We
were called to work, before the Fall, in imitation of God our Father.

Third, it means that we are like God. As *persons*, we have
reasoning intellects, free wills, and a unique capacity to love.

Furthermore, God made our nature unlike any other. As humans, we find ourselves somewhere between the angels and beasts, with physical bodies and rational souls. Angels can love but not reproduce; animals can reproduce but without love. However, we humans have a truly unique capacity to do both in the reproductive act of marital love, the covenantal source of interpersonal communion and family life.

+ Who in my life needs to hear how important and sacred life is? How could I make them feel true worth?

Lord God, what a privilege it is to be created as a human being! Let me develop a stronger awareness of the sacredness of human life, the true value of work, and the gift of marital love.

Made in the Image of God

"For those whom he foreknew he also predestined to
be conformed to the image of his Son, in order that he
might be the firstborn of many brethren."

—Romans 8:29

There's lots of talk about the importance of a good self-image these days. Some say it's a false problem; it doesn't really matter. I disagree. It does matter—a great deal. But we're going about it the wrong way. It's not the problem that is false but the so-called solutions. What we need isn't to create good self-images for everyone but to believe that everyone is created in God's image.

The profound truth about God creating us in his "image and likeness" first appears in Genesis, but in a very simple way. The next occurrence of the phrase, in Genesis 5:3, when Adam fathered a son "in his own likeness, after his image," plainly refers to a father-son relationship. More than a mere creature, Adam was endowed with the grace of divine sonship. From the first moment of his existence, Adam stood in the presence of God, as a son before his loving Father.

This not something to take for granted; the difference between Creator and creature is immeasurably vast. For us to have a good self-image, we have to develop the proper understanding and appreciation of what God's grace really accomplishes in us, and how much we need it. By nature, we are God's creatures and servants, but by grace, we are elevated to become his beloved children.

+ Are there areas in my life that need to be conformed to Christ's image? What step can I take during this Lent to create this change?

God, compared to your inexhaustible and infinite nature, humans are like little pieces of dust. But you still choose to infuse us with grace, which enables us to live as your adopted sons and daughters now and forever. Let me never take that for granted!

WEDNESDAY | WEEK ONE

Remember to Rest

"So God blessed the seventh day and hallowed it,
because on it God rested from all his work which he had
done in creation."

—Genesis 2:3

God not only "rested on the seventh day," he "blessed...and hallowed it." The seventh day doesn't signify God's exhaustion but rather his exuberance in calling his children to the end for which he made us: to rest in our Father's blessing and holiness, now and for all eternity.

God meant the Sabbath to be a joy for Israel, here and now. Isn't it odd that God has to command us to be blessed? From the beginning, God knew what we needed to be fulfilled, and so he provided it, as it were, "in the beginning." The Sabbath thus serves to remind us that our fulfillment requires something more than what we can obtain by our own natural labor or in our earthly life. That's why Israel had to "remember the Sabbath," so that, by renewing the covenant with their Father, they might continually rediscover how much he can be trusted to provide all that is needed, including what it takes to keep his laws.

In marking the end of God's work, the Sabbath also points to the ultimate end of man's royal work and priestly worship: eternal life in heaven. Our goal is to share God's Sabbath rest. Nothing less with do, at least as far as God is concerned. The Father commands us to be saints in order to enjoy communion with him forever. Thus, we must always do our temporal work with our eternal end in view.

+ What Christ endured on the cross makes it possible for me to truly rest. Is there a concern I have that I could let go of so I can rest in him?

Father, you knew from the beginning how important rest was, and you provided the Sabbath as a weekly reminder. Help me to rest from my work, knowing that this keeps me focused on my true goal: communion with you for all eternity.

THURSDAY | WEEK ONE

Jesus, the New Adam

"The LORD God formed man of dust from the ground,
and breathed into his nostrils the breath of life; and he
became a living soul."
—Genesis 2:7

God first formed Adam from the ground. Adam's name points to his role as father of the human race. God then "breathed into his nostrils the breath of life." God is depicted as directly breathing his own spirit into Adam. The Church fathers took this to mean that from his first breath, Adam was endowed with the Holy Spirit, not just a rational soul. Gazing out through the eyes of faith, he took his first step as a child of God, into the beauty of Eden, fully alive with the Spirit of divine sonship. Not a bad way to begin life, wouldn't you say?

But God had another surprise for Adam. "While he slept, [God] took one of his ribs and closed up its place with flesh…and made it into a woman and brought her to the man" (Genesis 2:21–22). Truly, Yahweh had saved his best for last—and Adam knew it. Holding nothing back, Adam let the whole world hear how he felt about this wondrous splendor: "This at last is bone of my bones and flesh of my flesh; she shall be called Woman, because she was taken out of Man" (Genesis 2:23).

What a glorious scene! Can you imagine a better opening to the family drama of salvation history? The sights and sounds of Adam's passion that are revealed here, pure and simple, prefigure the future—and even purer—passion of Jesus, the new Adam. Jesus offered the sacrifice of himself for his bride, the Church. In his dying breath he gave us his Spirit. From his pierced side there flowed living water and blood. From the deep sleep of his death came for the New Eve, who stood at his side, close to his heart.

+ What sacrifice could I make during Lent to show my love for the Church?

Lord Jesus, thank you for sacrificing yourself for your bride, the Church. Reflecting on creation's story gives the first glimpse of your tremendous love for us, and your passion and death only confirms it.

Paradise Lost

"And they heard the sound of the LORD God walking in
the garden in the cool of the day, and the man and his
wife hid themselves from the presence of the LORD God
among the trees of the garden."

—Genesis 3:8

When Adam and Eve sinned, they tried to hide from God and immediately began making excuses. But how did God respond? He decreed severe consequences, including increased pain in childbearing, toilsome tilling of the soil, and ultimately death. However, the Father responded to the disobedience of our first parents in the most loving way possible. Even though these human creatures had broken their covenant with him—the sacred family bond of trust—the Father promised a Savior (and a Woman) who would crush the head of Satan.

"Because you have done this, cursed are you above all the cattle, and above all wild animals; upon your belly you shall go, and dust you shall eat all the days of your life. I will put enmity between you and the woman, and between your seed and her seed; he shall bruise your head, and you shall bruise his heel" (Genesis 3:14–15).

This oracle is known as the "first gospel" (protoevangelion). It is the hinge on which the rest of salvation history turns. And it continues to turn, from one covenantal period to the next, as God's people await the fulfillment of this glorious promise.

+ Like Adam and Eve, when I hide from God, I lose all sense of peace. How long has it been since I went to confession? Could I make confession a regular part of my Lenten journey?

God, Adam and Eve wasted a lot of time and energy justifying themselves at the expense of each other. How often do we do the same? You continue to love us in spite of broken covenants and disobedience, and you provide a way of redemption through your beloved Son.

SATURDAY | WEEK ONE

Slaves or Sons?

"And on the seventh day God finished his work which
he had done, and he rested on the seventh day from
all the work which he had done. So God blessed the
seventh day and hallowed it, because on it God rested
from all his work which he had done in creation."

—Genesis 2:2–3

Since man was created on the sixth day, his first full day would
have been the Sabbath. Curious, isn't it, that God called man to
rest even before he began to work? Personally, I think God was
trying to teach us an important lesson from the very beginning
about faith.

The danger of unbelief is subtle: We often prefer to labor as
slaves rather than work as sons trusting in our Father's grace. We
are tempted to reduce the Father's law to a servile code. Jesus thus
reminds us, "The Sabbath was made for man, not man for the
Sabbath" (Mark 2:27).

This sheds a whole new light on Creation. God's intention is so
pure. Everything he does is for our good, our joy. God could have
made everything in an instant, effortlessly. He didn't need six days
to create, nor one to recuperate. Truly, God didn't need to make

anything at all, period. When he decided to bring the human race into existence, it wasn't due to boredom or loneliness. The Father, the Son, and the Spirit have shared the most intimate family life and love from all eternity. They didn't need more fellowship, and God didn't lack any glory.

God created and redeemed us to share in the grace and glory of divine sonship. The Lord worked for six days and then rested on the seventh for our sake, not his, as a healthy pattern for us to imitate, one that fits our nature perfectly. After all, the Father should know.

+ What specific activities or habits would make Sunday a day of rest for me? What is one thing I could refrain from doing? What could I do differently?

Heavenly Father, you have called me to rest from my work, just as you rested from yours. Help me to work as your child, not choosing to labor as a slave but always trusting in your grace. During this time of Lent, let me prepare ahead of time and be especially mindful to make Sunday a day of rest.

Week Two

| THE OBEDIENCE OF NOAH AND ABRAHAM |

We see how much we are called to be our brothers' and sisters' true keepers when we discover the meaning of God's covenant love. The body of Christ is the family of God, with each parish living out one small reflection of that divine love. Are we striving to be obedient to God's call, following the example of Noah and Abraham? Are we trying to live out the image and likeness of God? Or are we blaming others, while excusing ourselves, even with the best of motives? This week, as we seek to perceive more clearly the Father's continuing pursuit of his people, let's resolve to allow his love to penetrate our hearts more deeply.

SUNDAY | WEEK TWO

Broken Hearts, Broken Homes

"When man looks into his own heart he finds that
he is drawn toward what is wrong and sunk in many
evils which cannot come from his good creator. Often
refusing to acknowledge God as his source, man has
also upset the relationship which should link him to his
last end; and at the same time he has broken the right
order that should reign within himself as well as between
himself and other men and all creatures."

—*Gaudium et Spes*, 13

What images come to mind when you hear the word *family*? Many people think of Mom, apple pie, bedtime stories, and summer vacations. Others might think of in-laws, arguments, and mortgage payments. In reality, family includes both sets of images—and everything else in between. And that goes for God's family as well.

Salvation history reveals sin literally as a broken home. As members of God's family, we begin to understand that sin is primarily a broken *relationship*, not just broken *rules*. Like rebellious children who want to go their own way, we've all turned away from God many times during our lives. Even as we do, he keeps right on loving us, calling us back to himself, disciplining us in love as only a perfect Father can, and keeping his promises nonetheless.

These broken bonds began with the first union of man and woman. By eating the forbidden fruit, Adam and Eve repudiated their trust in the one who made them. What were the consequences? Look around. We live in a world riddled with fear, shame, anger, murder, pain, depression, isolation, alienation, and death. Not a pretty picture, is it?

+ What small way could I make someone in my family happier today?

Heavenly Father, it is not surprising there are so many broken homes and unhappy families. And yet you still love us and call us back into relationship with you and with each other. Jesus's sacrifice on the cross restores us to your family and makes it possible to create happy families here on earth too.

MONDAY | WEEK TWO

The Destructive Power of Envy

"The LORD said to Cain, 'Why are you angry, and why
has your countenance fallen? If you do well, will you not
be accepted? And if you do not do well, sin is lurking at
the door; its desire is for you, but you must master it.'"

—Genesis 4:6–7

As a tiller of the ground, Cain brought an offering of fruit from the
ground to the Lord, while Abel sacrificed firstlings from his flock.
God accepted Abel's gift but rejected Cain's. Cain was furious, but
God gave him some sound advice (see Genesis 4:6–7).

Did Cain learn a simple lesson, go back to the drawing board,
and try a second time? No. Cain apparently preferred an alto-
gether different sort of sacrifice. He lured his brother out to the
field and murdered him. In so doing, Cain bore the malicious fruit
that Satan had planted as a seed within our human nature.

It's important to note that Eve's firstborn didn't succumb to
a little fit of jealousy—he succumbed to the deadly sin of envy.
Technically speaking, jealousy seeks the good that is perceived in
another person, whereas envy resents it, and even seeks to destroy
it. Jealousy can be good or bad, but envy is only and always evil.
Scripture describes God as "jealous" (see Exodus 20:5), but never

envious; he wants us for himself—since he made us—but only for our good.

The same destructive power of envy that was at the root of Cain's sin is still at work in families and neighborhoods and workplaces everywhere today. The only remedy is abandoning ourselves to God's providence, trusting our heavenly Father to meet our needs and keep his promises to us.

+ When have I experienced the destructive power of envy? What were its consequences in my life, and how can I experience healing?

Thank you, God, that even though each generation continues to experience the destructive consequences of sin, you have invited us to be part of the body of Christ, and you have made it possible for your love to penetrate our hearts ever more deeply.

TUESDAY | WEEK TWO

A Covenant Renewed

"Noah was a righteous man, blameless in his generation;
Noah walked with God."

—Genesis 6:9

Chosen by the Father to embody—and deliver—the remnant of the human race, Noah was called to refound God's family, like a new Adam. Interestingly, the description of God's flood-judgment is notably similar to the pattern of divine creation in the opening chapters of Genesis. In both cases, a new world would emerge from the chaotic waters of the deep. After disembarking, Adam's divine commission was repeated for Noah: "Be fruitful and multiply, and fill the earth" (Genesis 9:1). God also restored Noah to Adam's former dominion over the beasts (see Genesis 9:2).

Finally, the Father renewed the creation covenant with Noah (see Genesis 9:9), revealing to him a rainbow as the sign of the new covenant (see Genesis 9:13). Clearly the flood account is presented as a re-creation event. Even Noah's name is significant: It means "rest" or "relief" (see Genesis 5:29), reflecting the Sabbath mandate. The Sabbath is the sign of God's creation with creation; the rainbow becomes the sign of God's renewed covenant with creation. God renews his covenant with Noah as a husband—but even more than husband, God renews his covenant with Noah as father of a household. There are four married couples on the ark, and Noah is the head of the covenant family.

+ Noah knew how to prepare, and he knew how to let go. How can this Lent become a time of preparation for me? What can I let go of?

God, how grateful I am for your renewed covenant. Every time I see a rainbow, it serves as a reminder of your faithfulness and love. I pray that I can follow in Noah's steps and walk with you.

The Obedience of Faith

"Go from your country and your kindred and your
father's house to the land that I will show you."
—Genesis 12:1

What if God asked you to pack up your belongings, leave your
home and your people and travel almost a thousand miles to an
unknown destination? I'm sure a host of questions would cross
your mind. *How can I be sure this crazy idea is really from God and
not just my imagination? Assuming we survive the journey, how will
we find a place to live and a new job to provide for our needs? How can
I know if the people who live there are hostile or friendly to people of our
race?* And what if you heard this message when you were seventy-
five years old? That's just what happened to Abram.

We tend to shrug our collective shoulders and think, *So what's
the big deal? This old guy was probably living in a tent in the middle
of nowhere.* But the reality was far different. Abram lived in Ur,
the Las Vegas of the ancient world, a city known for its prosperity.
And Abram himself was a rich man. In that case, we might think,
*Maybe God is finally showing some sense by going to a rich city to find
a man of power and wealth to conquer the world by force.* Such a
conclusion would miss God's intentions entirely.

God essentially told Abram, "Leave this rich, powerful city and go to a land you've never seen. Leave your people. Leave all your real estate holdings." And Abram obeyed. What incredible faith! Through this one faithful man, God was able to father the growing family of God.

+ What new direction is God calling me to consider? What will it take for me to courageously obey?

Abram's faith was truly amazing, Lord! I pray that my trust in you will increase this Lent so that when I hear you calling me to a new direction in my life, I will have the faith to obey you wholeheartedly.

Three Incredible Promises

"I will make of you a great nation, and I will bless
you, and make your name great, so that you will be a
blessing."

—Genesis 12:2

God made incredible promises to Abram that seemed to more
than compensate for his tangible losses. And although God waited
much longer to fulfill them than Abram wanted, he kept every one
of his promises. In his consuming desire to father a people to be
his own, God patiently worked in the life of this one man of faith,
as if tending a garden that would produce abundant fruit for all
humankind.

The Father gave Abram three unconditional promises: first, to
make of him a great nation; second, to make his "name" great; and
third, to bless "all the families of the earth" through him.

The first promise concerned land and nationhood. Any people
who didn't own land could never be a nation, great or otherwise.
God promised to make Abram's descendants the national occu-
pants of a vast amount of land where they would live and serve
the one God.

The second promise concerned Abram's name. The Hebrew
word for name also refers to a dynasty or kingdom, which carries

the notion of political power. Effectively, God planned to make Abram's nation a kingdom that would rule other nations.

The third promise concerned God's fatherly blessing of all the nations issuing from the seed of Abram. God didn't explain exactly what form this blessing would take, but it represents the climax of God's family plan and purpose for calling Abram.

+ What promises in the Bible mean the most to me and why?

Dear God, thank you for being a Father who keeps his promises—every one of them!

FRIDAY | WEEK TWO

Laugh at the Impossible
"Is anything too hard for the LORD?"
—Genesis 18:14

Fourteen years later, when Abram, now known as Abraham, was ninety-nine years old, God told him that he would father a son by Sarah. And how did the illustrious father of faith respond? He fell on his face and laughed!

As Abraham sat at the door of his tent, three strangers paid him a visit. While they rested under the oak trees, Abraham asked Sarah to whip up a fresh batch of bread. Then he picked out a tender calf from his herd and gave it to his servant to prepare. When all was ready, he laid the food before his heavenly guests.

When they had eaten their fill, the visitors asked, "Where is Sarah your wife?" When Abraham told them she was in the tent, they said, "The Lord said, 'I will surely return to you in the spring, and Sarah your wife shall have a son'" (Genesis 18:10). Wanting to hear what these honored guests had to say, Sarah had her ear glued to the tent door. Just like Abraham, she laughed to herself in disbelief (see v. 12).

The Father's ears are ever sensitive to our slightest chuckle or softest whisper. One of the heavenly visitors asked Abraham why

Sarah laughed and questioned his promise, saying, "Is anything to hard for the Lord?" (verse 14).

And it was true—at long last God opened a small window of heaven to pour out his blessings in the form of a baby boy. Isaac was born to Sarah the following spring, just as the Lord had promised.

+ What impossible situation am I facing right now? How can I face it with joy, and even laughter?

Lord, sometimes your promises are hard to believe; they seem too good to be true, or impossible to bring about. Help me to remember that nothing is too hard for you!

God Will Provide

"God will provide himself the lamb for a
burnt offering, my son."
—Genesis 22:8

God tested Abraham in a dramatic way, telling him to take his
son, his only son Isaac, whom he loved, and go to Moriah (a three-
day journey) and offer him there as a burnt offering (see Genesis
22:1–2). Amazingly, Abraham obeyed without question. His
obedience was rewarded when God intervened at the last minute,
saying, "Do not lay your hand on the lad…for now I know that
you fear God, seeing you have not withheld your son, your only
son, from me" (v. 12).

Two thousand years later, this same God called his only beloved
Son to go to that same place (Calvary is one of the hills of Moriah)
to die on a cross for our sake. The Son of God climbed that hill,
just like Isaac, for the Lord did provide the Lamb of God who
takes away the sins of the world.

This time it wasn't Isaac carrying the wood; it was Jesus carrying
the wooden cross. But this time the only sound from heaven was
complete and utter silence, as the soldiers hammered the nails,
then hoisted the cross and dropped it into place. The Father's only
beloved Son was thus sacrificed like a lamb for our sins.

When God saw that Abraham had not withheld his only son, he swore to bless all nations through Abraham's seed. Since the blessing of a father is reserved for his family, this oath is nothing less than God's pledge to restore the human race as his worldwide family. The establishment of the Catholic Church represents nothing less than the historic fulfillment of God's sworn covenant to Abraham.

+ What extreme measures is God calling me to take to weed out any unfaithfulness in my own life?

Lord, you have gone to extreme measures to demonstrate your faithfulness to us. When we respond to you with radical trust and obedience, our rewards are great!

Week Three

| THE EXODUS |

God's chosen people abandoned the law he gave them. For their sins, the temple was destroyed, and they were exiled in Babylon. But God, in his mercy, gathered them back, even anointing a pagan king to shepherd them and rebuild the temple. Being rich in mercy, he promised that David's kingdom would last forever, that David's son would be his Son and rule all nations. In Jesus, God keeps that promise.

Moses lifted up the serpent as a sign of salvation. Jesus was lifted up on the cross, to draw all people to himself. Those who refuse to believe in this sign of the Father's love condemn themselves—as the Israelites in their infidelity brought judgment upon themselves.

But God did not leave Israel in exile, and he does not want to leave any of us dead in our transgressions. We are God's handiwork, saved to live as his people in the light of his truth.

As we begin week three of this season of repentance, let us again behold the Pierced One (see John 19:37), and rededicate ourselves to living the "good works" that God has prepared us for.

God's Power, Not Ours

"Two nations are in your womb,
and two peoples, born of you, shall be divided;
the one shall be stronger than the other,
the elder shall serve the younger."

—Genesis 25:23

Advanced in years and fearful his son might marry a Canaanite, Abraham sent his servant to the land of Ur, Abraham's hometown, to find a wife for Isaac. God led the servant to Rebekah, the daughter of Abraham's brother. This woman of unusual faith and courage agreed to leave her family and hastily set off for a distant land.

In due time, Rebekah conceived twins. When the two sons struggled together within her womb, the Lord told her that two nations were in her womb, and that the elder son would serve the younger. But even though God had earmarked Jacob to be Isaac's heir, Isaac loved his older son, Esau, the best, while Rebekah favored Jacob. Isaac wanted to bless his elder son, while God intended to bless the younger.

This is a subplot that runs throughout the Bible: The younger is chosen over the elder. God chooses the weaker, younger brother to show that his plans are fulfilled through *his* power, not that of men.

> + Where do I feel particularly weak these days? How could I rely more tangibly on God's strength?

Heavenly Father, so often your ways are not our ways. How important it is to recognize that it is your power that counts, not our efforts apart from you. Lent is a good time to reflect on our weakness and your strength.

MONDAY | WEEK THREE

No Obstacles for God

"God has made me forget all my hardship…. God has
made me fruitful in the land of my affliction."

—Genesis 41:51–52

After many intervening years filled with illicit sex, violence, and
intrigue, the book of Genesis ends with the story of Joseph. The
son of Israel's old age, Joseph was clearly his father's favorite,
provoking strong resentment and envy in his older brothers. They
hated him even more when their father gave him a special coat,
and out of jealousy his brothers plotted together and sold him
into slavery. God's family had once again taken a very wrong turn.
How could the Father possibly turn this betrayal to good?

As a slave owned by one of the most powerful men in Egypt,
Joseph was put in charge of all Potiphar owned. However, Potiphar's
wife, angry that Joseph would not give in to her advances, accused
Joseph of attempted rape. Furious of this presumed treachery,
Potiphar threw Joseph into prison.

The Lord was with Joseph in prison, showing him his steadfast
love. Joseph's ability to interpret dreams and his wise counsel saves
the Egyptians and many others from famine. As a result Joseph
is released from prison and becomes prime minister over all of
Egypt.

Difficult circumstances never seem to deter the Father from carrying out his plans and keeping his promises. He is especially creative whenever adversity strikes, even showing a flair for the dramatic. We might even wonder whether God doesn't sometimes arrange severe obstacles in order to make his divine power more unmistakable.

+ What is the most difficult thing in my life right now? Am I focusing on God's power or on the difficulty?

Lord, you are aware of the difficult circumstances I face. Help me to have faith that these are not obstacles that keep you from accomplishing your purposes in my life. The more severe the difficulty appears, the more your divine power shines through.

TUESDAY | WEEK THREE

Forgiveness Reunites

"As for you, you meant evil against me; but God meant
it for good, to bring it about that many people should be
kept alive, as they are today. So do not fear; I will provide
for you and your little ones."

—Genesis 50:20–21

All that Joseph predicted came true. When famine struck and the
need for food became acute, Joseph opened the storehouses and
sold grain to the Egyptians. Food was scarce in Canaan as well.
Israel's family was in danger of starving, so Joseph's father sent his
older sons to buy grain in Egypt. When Joseph's ten half-brothers
fell on their faces before the prime minister to beg for bread, none
of them recognized the grown-up Joseph arrayed in splendor.

Joseph recognized them immediately but showed no sign of it.
Instead, he pulled a series of tricks on them, causing them distress.
As a result of their troubles, they uttered among themselves a
heartfelt repentance for their sin against Joseph so many years
before.

What follows is one of the most poignant scenes in all litera-
ture, when Joseph broke down in tears and revealed himself to his
brothers and forgiving them. When Israel heard that his son was

not only alive but living in splendor, he brought all of his family to Egypt. Pharaoh directed Joseph to give them the best land, so they settled in Goshen, a prime piece of Egyptian real estate.

The Father had kept his promises to provide for his people and to prosper them in the midst of plenty or poverty. Would he also keep his promise to bring them out of Egypt and give them a land of their own? We shall see that God's timetable rarely corresponds to our own.

+ How can Jesus's actions during his passion make a difference in how I respond to being wronged? Whom do I need to forgive today?

Lord, you too endured cruel treatment at the hands of those who meant evil toward you, and, like Joseph, you forgave them. You knew that God meant it all for good. Teach me to have your perspective when I feel betrayed and misused by others.

God Uses Adversity

"Know of a surety that your descendants will be
sojourners in a land that is not theirs, and will be slaves
there, and they will be oppressed for four hundred years;
but I will bring judgment on the nation which they
serve, and afterward they shall come out with
great possessions."
—Genesis 15:13–14

After Joseph's generation had gone the way of all human flesh, the descendants of Israel continued to be fruitful and multiply greatly, "so that the land was filled with them" (Exodus 1:7). In a matter of centuries, Jacob's twelve sons had grown to become the twelve tribes of Israel. But they weren't a unified nation yet, and things went from bad to worse.

A new pharaoh eventually came to power who viewed former allies as a potential threat to his own political power. This new pharaoh set heavy taskmasters over the Israelites, and the Egyptians made their lives miserable with all kinds of hard work.

Next Pharaoh ordered the midwives to kill all of the Hebrew male children at birth (see Exodus 1:1–16). These women, however, feared God and refused to obey. When Pharaoh found out that his commands were not being carried out, he questioned the midwives. They gave him a clever answer: the Hebrew women were so vigorous that they delivered before a midwife could even arrive. And God blessed the midwives and gave the families of their own.

The Lord had warned Abraham in a dream that his descendants would be enslaved for four hundred years (see Genesis 15:13–16). Yet the Father didn't see this as a serious obstacle for this realization of his family plans. In fact, the biblical drama shows how God always uses adversity to demonstrate his love and power, to prove that he keeps his promises now matter what—or who—stands in the way.

+ What opposition am I facing? Am I trusting God's promises or living with unhappiness and worry?

Dear God, no matter who or what stands against me, your plans for me are never in jeopardy. I can always count on you to keep your promises!

God's Plan for Moses

"God remembered his covenant with Abraham, with
Isaac, and with Jacob. And God saw the sons of Israel,
and God knew their condition."

—Exodus 2:24–25

Adopted as a baby by Pharaoh's daughter, Moses was raised as
a favored member of Pharaoh's royal court. But when Moses
murdered an Egyptian he observed beating a Hebrew, Pharaoh
sought to kill Moses. Rejected by the Israelites and hunted by the
Egyptians, Moses fled. Even so, the fugitive was nestled securely
in the hands of a Father who would guide his footsteps, patiently
biding his time until his son was ready for the task ahead: the
rescue of God's family from bondage.

Moses escaped into the desert and stayed in the land of Midian,
where he hit it off with Jethro, a priest of Midian. Moses stayed
on with this prominent family (who happened to be relatives of
Abraham). Jethro gave Moses his daughter Zipporah as his wife,
who bore him a son named Gershom (see Exodus 2:16–22).

Meanwhile, back in Egypt, God heard the groanings of the
Israelite slaves and remembered his covenant with Abraham. God
had been working behind the scenes all along to accomplish his

purposes. And Moses, a man without a country, was to play a crucial role in God's plan to deliver Israel from bondage.

> + Who in my life might be placed there to free me from myself? And what role do you have for me to play in the lives of others?

Lord, you don't forget your people, and you don't forget me. You choose various individuals—often unlikely individuals—to fulfill your purposes.

An Unlikely Hero

"The Egyptians shall know that I am the LORD, when
I stretch forth my hand upon Egypt and bring out the
sons of Israel from among them."

—Exodus 7:5

God speaks to Moses from a burning bush, telling him that he has heard the cries of his enslaved people and promises to deliver them and bring them into the Promised Land. He reveals his plans to Moses, an unlikely hero who wasn't exactly filled with enthusiasm at the prospect of such an impossible mission. "Oh, my Lord, send, I pray, some other person" (Exodus 4:13). God finally agrees to let Moses and his brother Aaron act as a team to visit Pharaoh to request that he set the Israelites free.

When Pharaoh refuses to let the people go, God responds by sending ten famous plagues to Egypt, symbolizing God's judgment on the gods of Egypt. Even after nine plagues, though, Pharaoh's heart remains hardened. What finally breaks him is plague number ten: the death of his firstborn son (see Exodus 12:30–32), and he drives the people of Israel out of the land. God appears before Israel as a pillar of cloud by day and a pillar of fire by night. He leads his people out of Egypt and through the Red Sea.

St. Paul explains that this foreshadows the new covenant: Just as the Holy Spirit led Israel through the Red Sea under Moses, so we are baptized into Christ and the Spirit in the baptismal waters. Furthermore, Moses gave the people heavenly bread and supernatural drink in the form of miraculous manna and water from a rock; Jesus gives us the Eucharist (see 1 Corinthians 10:1–4).

+ Has there been a time when I wished God would pick someone other than me to do some act of service? How does this relate to my journey through Lent?

Dear God, the story of Moses and the Israelites paints a vivid picture of your love and power on behalf of those you come to save. You were on a rescue mission, and you could not be stopped. Against all odds, you freed the Hebrews from their slavery, and you will free me from any bondage too!

True Liberation

"Who is like you, O LORD, among the gods?
Who is like you, majestic in holiness,
terrible in glorious deeds, doing wonders?"
—Exodus 15:11

The Israelites had just witnessed one awesome demonstration of divine power after another. In every affliction, they were miraculously protected from harm. Surely they were now convinced that the God of Abraham, Isaac, and Jacob would meet their every need and keep every one of his promises. They celebrated by singing a rousing song of victory.

Unfortunately, their jubilation was short-lived. After three days' journey into the wilderness, they could find no water and began to murmur against Moses. The Father heard their cry and provided water. After six weeks, their stomachs rumbled with hunger and they complained loudly, even tempted to return to Egypt and their former bondage (see Exodus 16:3). Not exactly an attitude of faith or gratitude.

Through each of these crises of faith, we see God the Father full of compassion and ever ready to meet their needs. We see him faithful to his promises, even when his human family is ready to turn back to slavery. Like most of us, Israel had to learn about God's love the hard way.

God wasn't content with liberating Israel from mere physical slavery in Egypt. His goal wasn't to simply bring them into the Promised Land but to make them reliant on him alone. It's a lesson we're always learning, too: God loves us just as we are, but he loves us too much to leave us that way.

> + What does true liberation mean to me? Am I willing to allow God to exercise "tough love" in order to accomplish this in my life?

Lord, your divine compassion often feels like "tough love." You aren't willing to settle for anything less than radical surgery, without which we would remain enslaved internally to meaningless idols. Thank you for your continued care.

Week Four

| ISRAEL IN THE WILDERNESS |

God's desire is to deliver the Israelites from bondage and return them to the Promised Land. He is determined to fulfill his covenant promises, but first the Israelites, because of their rebellion and disobedience, must first wander in the wilderness.

Against all odds and by the Father's grace, Moses eventually succeeded in transforming Abraham's tribal family into the national family of God. Through this reluctant leader, the Lord reorganized and cared for his people. Despite their ongoing rebellions in the desert, they were eventually reunited behind a common purpose: to reclaim the ancestral inheritance that God had promised them.

The nation of Israel had a hard time finding its way out of the desert. But then, all of God's children, to this very day, experience the same struggle to see the promises of God the Father fulfilled in their lives. As we progress through Lent, may God give us the strength and courage to move forward, one step at a time.

A New Identity

"You have seen what I did to the Egyptians, and how
I bore you on eagles' wings and brought you to myself.
Now therefore, if you will obey my voice and keep my
covenant, you shall be…
a kingdom of priests and a holy nation."

—Exodus 19:3–6

Israel's future identity hung upon the biggest "if" in history: "*If* you
obey my voice and keep my covenant…" When Moses delivered
the word of the Lord, the people seemed ready to obey. "All that
the Lord has spoken we will do" (Exodus 19:8). Little did they
know what they were getting themselves into. God was declaring
his intention to transform this complaining bunch into a kingdom
of priests. They were to extend the Father's unifying and universal
rule to the whole world.

The Ten Commandments gave this ragtag outfit of twelve
loosely knit tribes a new identity and revealed a radically new way
of living. We can imagine God speaking to them of an awesome
calling: "You will be a kingdom of priests. You won't rule through
political power or military strength, as the Egyptians do, but
through wisdom and righteousness and holiness. Through holy

lives and prayer and sacrifice, you will earn the right to be heard and believed and followed. You will draw the nations to return to me freely, but only if you put all your trust in me and meet me face-to-face and hear me speak my law of love."

God's message was clear: Throughout all of Israel, God wanted every tent to be a tabernacle, every hearth an altar, every father a priest, every firstborn son a deacon, and every family a domestic church. The nation was to be a kingdom of priests…if only they would forsake the idols of Egypt and place their wholehearted trust in God.

+ How do I define myself? Does my life reflect what God says is important?

God, in our day too, you look for those who live holy lives, lives of prayer and sacrifice. During this Lenten season, let me trust you with all my heart and obey your law of love.

MONDAY | WEEK FOUR

A Privilege and a Responsibility

"Behold the blood of the covenant which the LORD has
made with you in accordance with all these words."
—Exodus 24:8

According to the ancient Hebrew outlook, the symbolic meaning
of the blood-sprinkling upon both altar and people was twofold:
Positively, it symbolized the blood covenant between God and
Israel; negatively, the shed blood signified a solemn curse that
Israel placed itself under by swearing the covenant oath.

At the Father's invitation, Moses accompanied Aaron, Nadab,
Abihu, and the seventy elders up the mountain. These leaders saw
God and ate and drank before him. From the ancient Hebrew
perspective, covenant meals like this conveyed a twofold symbolic
meaning: the intimate family ties between covenant parties, and
the awesome responsibilities that both parties assumed. The meal
was the sign of the covenant blessing of communion, while the
sacrificial victims signified the covenant curse that would befall
Israel if they went back on their sworn oath. A similar twofold
meaning is also present in the Holy Eucharist, which Jesus instituted to be the sign of the New Covenant—as both a sacrifice and
a meal | Which the Passover and the Sinai covenant ritual both
foreshadow (see 1 Corinthians 10:1–22; 11:26–32).

+ Do I see Mass as a weekly duty, or as a privilege I want to enjoy as often as possible?

Lord Jesus, as I partake of the Eucharist, let me delight in being part of your family, and let me also remember the responsibilities that come with such a privilege!

TUESDAY | WEEK FOUR

The Great Physician

"For it was fitting that we should have such a high
priest, holy, blameless, unstained, separated from sinners,
exalted above the heavens. He has no need, like those
high priests, to offer sacrifices daily, first for his own sins
and then for those of the people; he did this once for all
when he offered up himself."

—Hebrews 7:27

In worshiping the golden calf, the Israelites once again pledged their allegiance to the Egyptian idolatry they had been brought out of. They chose the lesser gods of this world rather than the highest good offered by God—the gift of himself to his people in covenant communion forever. By worshiping the golden calf, Israel committed a heinous crime, a desecrating sacrilege, an act of covenant apostasy that profaned the holy name of God and released the dreaded curses.

To remedy the situation, Israel was commanded to offer daily sacrifices. God knew that they were hopelessly ensnared in the idolatrous ways of Egypt. God knew that something far more radical was needed to cut out this defiling disease. But was the patient ready to undergo such radical surgery? God's answer was

No, not yet. The Great Physician decided to postpone surgery until "the fullness of time" when "God sent forth his Son...born under the law" (Galatians 4:4), that is, under its "curse" (see Galatians 3:10), which Christ alone could bear.

Once again, God showed Israel his fatherly foresight and merciful ingenuity. By a holy mixture of justice and goodness, God elected certain figures (Moses, Aaron, and the Levites) to bear Israel's curse *symbolically* until he sent the One who was both willing and worthy to bear it *redemptively*.

+ What might have an unhealthy hold on me? Is it food, drink, or too much time on the Internet? What can I "fast" from this Lent?

Just like the Israelites, Lord, you long to set me free from all my earthly addictions. You know how easy it is for your children to fall back into bondage. You are a wise and loving Father, and I thank you for sending your Son as the true cure.

Rules and Rebellion

"For the LORD will again take delight in prospering you,
as he took delight in your fathers, if you obey the voice
of the LORD your God, to keep his commandments and
his statutes which are written in this book of the law, if
you turn to the LORD your God with all your heart and
with all your soul."
—Deuteronomy 30:9–10

After forty long years, the first generation of Israelites had died off, except for Moses and the two courageous spies, Joshua and Caleb. During this time, the second generation was being taught by their Levitical tutors and hopefully rehabilitated from the sinful ways of their parents. But patterns of bad behavior die hard, especially when they're transmitted from parent to child, so the outcome of their probationary period remained something of an unanswered question: Would the second generation succeed where the first had failed?

Israel finally reached the eastern border of the Promised Land on the plains of Moab. This was where God would put the second generation to the test, just as he had done with the first at Sinai. They didn't know it, but the entire future of Israel was hanging in the balance.

To make a long (and sordid) story short, the second generation fell into idolatry at Beth-peor about as hard as their parents did at Sinai. Moses, who was near the end of his life, witnessed his last forty years of labor seemingly undone. What was left for him to do but to sit down and dictate his last will and testament? We call these five books Deuteronomy, and they served as the covenant rule for regulating God's rebellious son, Israel, and functioned as its national constitution ("the book of the Torah") until Jesus's coming.

+ How do I view God's rules? With loving obedience or as roadblocks to freedom?

Father, you stoop down to the level of your wayward children, providing them with laws to teach them how to grow up and become holy until you were ready to send your Son. Help me to obey you with joy, trusting that you know what's best.

The New Moses

"For the law was given through Moses;
grace and truth came through Jesus Christ."
—John 1:17

Jesus saw himself as the new Moses, giving a New Covenant to reconstitute a new Israel. Moses ascended the mountain to get God's Old Covenant law, whereas Jesus went up the mountain to give the New Covenant law, the Sermon on the Mount. Moses delivered the Ten Commandments to the people, along with curse threats, while Christ gave a law full of God's promised blessings (the Beatitudes). Moses offered himself as a substitute to take away Israel's temporal penalty, while Jesus died on the cross to remove our eternal punishment by reconciling us to the Father. Moses fashioned a national church government from twelve chiefs of the twelve tribes, along with the seventy elders. Jesus took twelve disciples and told them they would sit on the twelve thrones and rule the twelve tribes of Israel.

Only through Christ would the family of God finally be set free from the bondage to sin and idolatry. Jesus leads us out of the bondage of sin just as Moses led the Israelites out of the bondage of Egypt. Just as Moses gave their ancestors manna from heaven, so Jesus himself is the heavenly manna, the true bread of life. As for the Passover, Christ is the firstborn Son who is slain (see 1 Corinthians 5:7). The purpose of sharing the holy sacrifice of the Eucharist is to unite us as God's family, a communion that is actualized by eating the Passover Lamb of the New Covenant.

+ How hungry am I for Jesus? What steps do I need to take to increase my appetite for the true Bread from heaven?

God our Father, thank you for setting this glorious plan of salvation into action! Through your Son, we have true freedom from bondage and a full membership in your family. Help me to see Jesus's great gift in a new way this Lent.

From Faithfulness to Forgetfulness

"And Joshua the son of Nun was full of the spirit of
wisdom, for Moses had laid his hands upon him; so
the sons of Israel obeyed him, and did as the LORD had
commanded Moses."

—Deuteronomy 34:9

Because Moses had taken great care in grooming Joshua to be
his successor, Joshua was able to lead the people of Israel across
the Jordan River into the land of Canaan, beginning with the
conquest of Jericho, a Canaanite stronghold with virtually impreg-
nable walls (see Joshua 6).

Following the Lord's instructions, Joshua implemented a most
unusual battle plan. Instead of following the ancient custom of
deploying soldiers equipped with the weapons of siege warfare,
Joshua ordered the priests to lead the armies, carrying the ark of
the covenant out in front, with the twelve tribes following behind.
After six days of silently marching once around the city, they
were to march around it seven times on the seventh day, and the
priests had to blow their trumpets while the people shouted. This
unorthodox strategy worked perfectly, because the battle belonged
to the Lord.

After defeating Jericho, this early success went to the Israelites' head. Then followed the period of the judges, with Israel falling into one crisis after another. Israel kept following the same vicious cycle: sin, slavery, supplication, salvation, and surplus. Faithfulness would then beget fullness, which in turn begot flabbiness and forgetfulness. There would be another fall, followed by forgiveness and freedom. This cycle continued through a lengthy chain of twelve judges. Israel just never seemed to learn. But then are we any better or more proficient at following the ways of God?

+ What negative cycle can I choose to overcome? How can this Lent be a catalyst for increased faithfulness to God?

Oh, Father, too often I see the same patterns of sin in my life repeated over and over. I stumble and fall, confess my stubbornness and pride to you, obtain forgiveness—only to fall into the same thing again. I thank you for your patience toward the Israelites, and toward me!

SATURDAY | WEEK FOUR

Total Rest

"And I will appoint a place for my people Israel, and will
plant them, that they may dwell in their own place, and
be disturbed no more; and violent men shall afflict them
no more, as formerly...
and I will give you rest from all your enemies."
—2 Samuel 7:10–11

In addition to pastoral accommodations, Moses also introduced
two additional laws in Deuteronomy for regulating Israel during
its adolescent phase: the law of the king and the central sanctuary.
Both laws offer important keys for unlocking God's hidden plan
for Israel. They would also be eventually fulfilled in the Father's
covenant with the son of David. God's plan, in effect, was to build
an earthly model of his heavenly throne and temple.

The result of building the sanctuary was to be total rest. The
exact place is nowhere stipulated, though Jerusalem was clearly
meant. This achievement of "rest" and the construction of a temple
were seen in Israel (and in the entire ancient Near East) as a royal
accomplishment. Thus, Israel needed to find a righteous king who
met the Deuteronomic criteria of the "law of the king," to whom
God could give "rest" and the authorization to build a temple.

That's how God who is Spirit responds to the human desire for visible signs of his presence. In this instance, we see how the Father stoops down to his children's level in order to raise them up to his. However, at this point in Israel's history, God still had some more stooping to do.

+ What hard lessons have I learned when I've tried to make things happen on my own? What is my experience of true rest?

Lord, sometimes you must get tired of hearing me tell you the way I think things should work out. And sometimes, I think you finally give in and allow me to learn the hard way. This Lent, let me relinquish all that and experience the rest that only you can provide.

Week Five

| FROM KINGDOM TO EXILE |

David's faith allowed him to recognize the deeper import of God's promise: that his dynasty would be a universal kingdom. In fact, this worldwide decree was the means by which God would establish the corporate destiny of the human family. Through the Davidic covenant, he would give a constitution for all humankind, an international family charter offered freely to the nations.

For a brief time, the surrounding nations accepted this charter, much as Israel had initially said yes to God's call to be a kingdom of priests. And then Israel and the nations repudiated God's call. But we must not be too quick to condemn them: Sacrificing the lower goods of this world, setting our hearts on treasures in heaven, and carrying our crosses have never been easy and never will be. And such are the lessons of Lent.

Humble Means

"Thus says the LORD of hosts, I took you from the
pasture, from following the sheep, that you should be
prince over my people Israel."

—2 Samuel 7:8

God often achieves his most awesome victories in the humblest
ways: A childless old man leaves home without even knowing
where he's going; a threatened baby in a basket is set afloat on
a river; a shepherd boy armed with only a sling and five smooth
stones faces a giant. And who in their wildest imagination could
have foreseen that same shepherd boy being crowned kind of
Israel, thus paving the way for the carpenter who would be the
King of kings?

At age thirty, David—now a seasoned leader—became king over
all twelve tribes of Israel. He would reign for the next forty years.
Having established his throne at Jerusalem—no small feat—David
gathered his best warriors and set out to accomplish one task: to
bring back the ark of the covenant from Baal-judah, where it had
been kept since the Philistines had returned it to the Israelites.
After a mishap and delay of a few months, David succeeded.

During this time his behavior was as much like that of a priest as it was like that of a king. This was because, having captured Jerusalem, David had taken a giant step forward in realizing God's Abrahamic covenant plan: restoring his reign and rule over the entire human family through his chosen people. After all, God had initially wanted the people of Israel to be royal priests—not kings at the edge of a sword but kings who would rule through priestly service and teaching. David symbolized that intended role.

+ Who are the unlikely heroes in my life?

Heavenly Father, I'm sure David never dreamed that he would be a king! You have plans for me too that I could never imagine. All I need to do is trust you, and you will lead me.

Son of Promise

"And your house and your kingdom shall be made sure
for ever before me; your throne shall be
established for ever."

—2 Samuel 7:16

David said to Nathan the prophet, "I dwell in this beautiful house of cedar while the ark of God dwells in a tent" (see 2 Samuel 7:2). The king wanted permission to do what in the ancient Near East was a very royal-priestly thing: to build a temple.

Nathan at first consented. "Go, do all that is in your heart; for the Lord is with you" (v. 3). Then the word of the Lord came to the prophet that night, effectively saying, "Not so fast." God sent the prophet back to David with another message, words that unlocked a whole new covenant and contained God's plan to renew—and fulfill—the promise he had made to Abraham to restore the unity of the human family (see verses 9–11).

Nathan must have been up half the night, for God's promises to David continued: "When your days are fulfilled and you lie down with your fathers, I will raise up offspring after you...and I will establish his kingdom. He shall build a house for my name, and I will establish the throne of his kingdom forever. I will be his father, and he shall be my son" (2 Samuel 7:12–14).

Solomon was this son of promise. He clearly prefigured Jesus Christ, the eternal Prince of Peace: Son of David, king of Israel, temple builder, teacher of wisdom. Our belief in Christ's kingdom is built on this very cornerstone.

+ Am I willing to listen to what God might be saying to me through others the way David listened to Nathan?

Jesus, you are Lord of lords and King of kings. There's not a single square inch of creation that escapes your dominion. And as children of the King, you call us to be your servants and soldiers, to extend your reign into every corner of this world.

TUESDAY | WEEK FIVE

A Servant's Heart

"Who am I, O Lord GOD, and what is my house, that
thou has brought me thus far? And yet this was a small
thing in thy eyes, O Lord GOD; though has spoken also
of thy servant's house for a great while to come, and hast
shown me future generations."

—2 Samuel 7:18–19

Even though David longed to build a temple and rule as a priest-
king, God denied him this privilege. He promised to grant it to
the king's son instead. Wouldn't you think that David would be
disappointed?

Yet how do fathers who fail to accomplish some dream react
when they see their sons achieve it instead? They typically feel even
greater satisfaction, as demonstrated in David's reply in 2 Samuel
7:18–19, which might be paraphrased this way: "O God, you have
done all these glorious deeds and made this promise for my house.
You've pledged yourself to do great things for my dynasty. Yet all
of this is small in your eyes, since what you have really given me is
the covenant law for all nations, your entire human family. I can't
believe my ears. Who am I, your lowly servant, that you would do
this for me and my son?" The father's glee over God's generosity
to his son was unbounded.

The Father had accomplished these glorious deeds because David thought of himself as nothing but a servant. If you feel like small stuff, take heart: that qualifies you to play a role in God's plan. God has always been and still is looking for people who see themselves as lowly, who are humble before the Lord and who fear the Creator more than their fellow creatures. Such are the ones the Father will use to strengthen his human family and thus build the kingdom of heaven for his own name's sake.

+ What are some areas where I could use more humility? What is one thing I could do to be more humble?

Father, I want to have a servant's heart, like David had. When I feel insignificant or overlooked, help me to remember that I too have a role to play in your kingdom. Help me to learn humility this Lent!

A Rich Treasury

"Serve the LORD with fear,

with trembling rejoice,

...

Blessed are all those who take refuge in him."

—Psalm 2:11, 12

King David left one tangible legacy for all humankind: a rich treasury of psalms. These vignettes of agony and ecstasy, hate and love, despair and victory, scorn and praise capture this man's unusually sensitive nature as well as his gift with words and music. The so-called royal psalms offer an insightful commentary as to the real meaning of the Davidic covenant.

Psalm 2 is one of the best known of these psalms. David reflects on the nations and kings of the earth who conspire together against the Lord and his Messiah, refusing to be ruled by God through his representative king. But the Lord has been listening in on their communications all along...laughing at their schemes (see v. 6). God wasn't worried about the kings and princes of the earth banding together to overthrow his righteous law. They may have deceived themselves and deluded others, but the Father knew their wayward hearts and rebellious plans and would make it all come back on their own heads. Psalm 2 thus highlights a particular aspect of the Davidic covenant: a worldwide theocratic family under God's fatherly law. The rulers of the earth who refuse to serve and worship the one true God court disaster and ruin.

The other royal psalms are Psalm 72, Psalm 89, and Psalm 110. Like Psalm 2, these psalms point to the partial fulfillment of the Davidic covenant in Solomon and its perfect fulfillment in Christ.

+ How often do I immerse myself in the psalms? How can I allow them to point me more fully to Christ?

Lord, I'm grateful for the gift of the psalms. Not only was David a great warrior and king, he was also a poet who expressed deep truth and deep emotion. The royal psalms pointed the way to Christ long ago, and they are still relevant today to reveal him.

THURSDAY | WEEK FIVE

God's Broken Heart

"Against you, you only, have I sinned,
and done that which is evil in your sight,

...

Create in me a clean heart, O God,
and put a new and right spirit within me."

—Psalm 51:4, 10

For all his prowess, faith, and poetic talent, King David exhibited a weakness for women that proved to be his downfall. You can read the story in 2 Samuel 11. After sleeping with Bathsheba, the wife of Uriah, one of his chief military advisors, she discovered she was with child. Desperate to cover his tracks, David crafted a plot to have Uriah killed in battle. David was sinking deeper and deeper with each step: first adultery, then murder. As intended, Uriah was cut down in battle. After the customary mourning period, Bathsheba became David's wife and bore him a son.

David eventually repented, and the Lord spared his life. In the aftermath of this tragedy, the contrite king wrote Psalm 51, the most profound song of repentance in Scripture. David's life became more and more miserable, culminating in the death of his beloved son Absalom during a power struggle between them, and bringing the greatest sorrow of all to David's heart.

David's sorrow, however, only faintly reflected the broken heart of God. Because of his sin, the house of David had been splintered by envy, hatred, and lust for power. How would the Father keep his promise to establish an everlasting kingdom through David's son? God's grand design of fashioning a human family under his lordship may have been challenged, but it wasn't destroyed.

+ Do I really feel true sorrow for my sins? Or do I tend to try to justify my shortcomings?

Dear Lord, the effects of envy, lust, and hatred can have far-reaching and devastating consequences. None of us are immune to the temptations David faced, and it is only by your grace that we can withstand them. When I fall into sin, let me say with David, "Create a clean heart, O God, and put a new and right spirit within me."

A Wise Man's Fall From Grace

"For when Solomon was old his wives turned away his
heart after other gods, and his heart was not wholly true
to the Lord his God, as was the heart of
David his father."

—1 Kings 11:4

Against the vigorous protests of his older half-brothers, Solomon
assumed the throne as David's chosen heir. The Heavenly Father
presented the new king with a special coronation gift: "I will give
you anything you ask. Do you want wealth? Long life? Power?"
Solomon answered, "No. I want wisdom." This pleased God, and
he promised to give Solomon wisdom and everything else as well
(see 1 Kings 3:11–14).

Solomon's astounding wisdom was soon broadcast throughout
the world. Kings and queens traveled from Africa, Europe, and
every inhabited continent to behold this wondrous gift. And with
that wisdom, King Solomon set to work building the temple, a
mammoth undertaking in terms of design, labor, and materials.

But having restored the glory of his father's kingdom, Solomon
then proceeded to violate all three rules enumerated in the "law
of the king" in Deuteronomy 17: He became a tyrant like all the

other kings; he demanded large sums of gold from the people who came to hear God's law; and he married women from other nations who worshiped pagan gods. His rapid fall from grace continued with building idolatrous altars so he could worship the Canaanite deities Asherah and Baal as well as Yahweh.

This God would not allow. He sent enemies from within and without so that Solomon grew old watching his kingdom slip away. God promised, however, to give one tribe to Solomon's son, thus pledging to keep his promise to David in spite of Solomon's failures.

+ Is there a particular area where I no longer live wisely? What have the consequences of this been?

Dear God, there are many lessons to learn from the life of Solomon. Even though he was wise and blessed with everything one could want, he still allowed himself to be lured away from you, and he paid a high price for this. Yet you did not let his faithlessness deter you—you continued to keep your promises.

SATURDAY | WEEK FIVE

A Profound Conversion

"'Return, faithless Israel,' says the Lord. 'I will not look
at you in anger, for I am merciful,' says the Lord; 'I will
not be angry for ever.'"

—Jeremiah 3:12

The millennium prior to Christ proved to be a crucible of purification and refinement for God's family. The blackest year by far was 586 BC, when the Babylonian king, Nebuchadnezzar, burned Jerusalem and carried the Jews away into captivity for seventy years. God's covenant family appeared to have been extinguished. However, prophets like Isaiah, Jeremiah, and Ezekiel saw this as God's appointed period for purging and penance.

Lacking political sovereignty or military power, the Jews were constantly vanquished or tyrannized by Gentile powers, until finally Rome had its turn, conquering Jerusalem in 63 BC. Devoid of kings and prophets, even the priestly line became riddled with corruption and weakness. Yet, during this period of suffering, subjugation, and martyrdom, the Jews experienced a profoundly deep conversion to the Lord. In the absence of prophets and kings, the Jews had nothing to lean on but the Lord.

It was a time of waiting and trusting in the Father to fulfill his covenant promises, and it yielded some precious spiritual fruit.

Prayer was cultivated, worship was refined, and allegiance to God's law flourished as never before. For the first time in Israel's history, many Jews were awarded the crown of martyrdom by suffering and dying for their faith. This intense suffering transformed the Jews into a holy priesthood. They now saw themselves as living sacrifices, and the world as one immense altar.

+ What areas of suffering can transform me into a living sacrifice?

Sometimes, Father, I too feel like all the props are pulled out from under me. And yet, these times of emptiness and confusion can be very rich spiritually—if only I remember to lean on you and trust in your mercy.

Holy Week

| IT IS FINISHED |

This week is filled with anticipation. The new covenant that God promised to Jeremiah is made in the "hour" of Jesus—in his death, resurrection, and ascension to the Father's right hand.

The prophets said this new covenant would return Israel's exiled tribes from the ends of the world. Jesus, too, predicted that his passion would gather the dispersed children of God (see John 11:52). But he also promises to draw to himself, not only Israelites, but all men and women.

The new covenant is more than a political or national restoration. It is a universal spiritual restoration. In the "hour" of Jesus, sinners in every nation can return to the Father—to be washed of their guilt and given new hearts to love and serve him.

Troubled in his agony, Jesus didn't pray to be saved. Instead, he offered himself to the Father on the cross—as a living prayer and supplication. For this, God gave him dominion over heaven and earth. Where Jesus has gone we can follow—if we let him lead us. To follow Jesus means hating our lives of sin and selfishness. It means trusting in the Father's will, the law he has written in our hearts. Jesus's "hour" continues in the Eucharist, where we join our sacrifices to his, giving God our lives in reverence and obedience, confident he will raise us up to bear fruits of holiness.

As we enter Holy Week, let us once more resolve to give Christ dominion in our lives. Let us take up the cross he gives us, and confess with all our hearts, minds, and strength that truly this is the Son of God.

PALM SUNDAY

What Is Finished?

"Jesus our Lord…was put to death for our trespasses and
raised for our justification."

—Romans 4:25

I have a vivid recollection of a Sunday morning service back in
1982, when Kimberly and I were worshiping at a local evangel-
ical congregation. I was a seminarian at the time, preparing for
ministry. It was during Lent, and our favorite minister was in the
middle of a very exciting sermon on the meaning of Jesus's sacrificial death on the cross at Calvary.

Suddenly, he raised what sounded at first like a simple question: "In John 19:30, when Jesus cried, 'It is finished,' what did he
mean? To what does the *it* refer?" I immediately knew that Jesus's
words referred to the completion of our redemption; our salvation
was complete.

This preacher was an exceptional Scripture scholar, as well as
one of my favorite seminar professors, so I was taken aback when
he proceed to convincingly prove that Jesus could not possibly
have meant that. Then to my dismay, he candidly admitted that
he didn't have an adequate answer to his own question.

I don't remember hearing another word of his sermon. My
mind began racing in search of an answer. After we got home, the

books came out and I started searching. And I didn't stop for ten months. An answer finally came, long after graduation, during my first year as a pastor, while I was studying Scripture in preparation for a sermon on the "Lord's Supper," as we Presbyterians called it. I still recall that thrilling sense of discovery, after such a long time of research into several key biblical texts.

+ How well do I know the Bible? When Lent is over, how will I continue to deepen my understanding of God's Word?

Lord Jesus, you fulfilled every one of the promises made by your Father. Show me more fully what your sacrifice on the cross really means. I'm listening, Lord!

MONDAY | HOLY WEEK

Jesus, Our Passover Lamb

"He took a cup, and when he had given thanks he gave it
them, saying, 'Drink of it, all of you; for this is my blood
of the covenant, which is poured out for many for the
forgiveness of sins.'"

—Matthew 26:27–28

The first stage of my discovery process was studying the Old
Testament background to Jesus's Last Supper—the Jewish feast of
Passover. On the momentous feast of his last Passover, Jesus instituted the Eucharist in the Upper Room (see Matthew 26:27–28).
What an awesome moment: the firstborn Son and Lamb of God
fulfilled the Old Covenant Passover in himself, as a holy sacrifice
for our sins. And it served as the occasion when Jesus deliberately
announced the establishment of the New Covenant.

As I continued my hunt, I discovered that the Passover link
involved more than just the Eucharist. This is especially clear in
John's Gospel, where the entire succession of events, which began
with the Last Supper and ended with Jesus's crucifixion, reflects
the various themes of the Jewish Passover. For example, when
Jesus stood before Pilate, John notes that it was the sixth hour:
the time when the priests were beginning to slaughter lambs for

Passover (see John 18:33–37). John also calls attention to the fact that Jesus's bones remained unbroken, just as Moses had stipulated for the Passover lamb (see John 19:33, 36; Exodus 12:46).

Another connection is found in John 19:29, where "a sponge full of vinegar on hyssop" was held to Jesus's mouth. Hyssop was the branch prescribed in the Passover law for sprinkling the blood of the lamb (see Exodus 12:22). Finally, John also calls attention to the seamless garment that Jesus wore when the soldiers stripped him: symbolizing the official tunic worn by the high priest when sacrificing (see Exodus 28:4). Jesus, our Passover Lamb, is also our High Priest.

+ How can I deepen my understanding and experience of
   the Eucharist?

Jesus, you demonstrate that the Eucharist—our new Passover—and Calvary are inseparable; they are one and the same sacrifice. And what you began in the Upper Room with your disciples, you finished on the cross.

TUESDAY | HOLY WEEK

The Cup of Blessing

"The cup of blessing which we bless, is it not a
participation in the blood of Christ?"
—1 Corinthians 10:16

As I studied the ancient Jewish Passover liturgy, I learned that the seder meal was divided into four parts, which correspond to the four different cups that were served. The preliminary course consisted of a solemn blessing pronounced over the first cup of wine, which was followed by a dish of bitter herbs. Next the Passover narrative was recited, after which Psalm 113 was sung. Drinking the second cup of wine immediately followed.

Third, the main meal was served, consisting of lamb and unleavened bread, which proceeded the drinking of the third cup of wine, known as the "cup of blessing." Finally, the climax of the Passover came with the singing of Psalms 114—118 and drinking the fourth cup of wine, the "cup of consummation."

Many New Testament scholars see this pattern reflected in the Gospel narratives of the Last Supper. In particular, the cup that Jesus blessed and distributed is identified as the third cup of the Passover meal. Paul identifies this "cup of blessing" with the cup of the Eucharist (see 1 Corinthians 10:16).

+ Is there a Bible study group I might consider joining once Lent is over? Why might this be beneficial?

Heavenly Father, how grateful I am for the Eucharist! Help me to learn more about this "cup of blessing" and never take it (or you) for granted.

WEDNESDAY | HOLY WEEK

The Paschal Mystery Fulfilled

"Truly, I say to you, I shall not drink again of the fruit
of the vine until that day when I drink it new in the
kingdom of God."

—Mark 14:25

Instead of progressing immediately to the climax of the Passover
by drinking the fourth cup, the disciples and Jesus went to the
Mount of Olives (see Mark 14:26). For students of the Passover,
Jesus'sskipping the fourth cup is almost the practical equivalent of
a priest's omitting the words of consecration at Mass or forgetting
Communion! Why did Jesus choose not to drink the fourth cup?

There in Gethsemane, Jesus prayed, "My Father, if it be possible,
let this cup pass from me" (Matthew 26:39). What cup was Jesus
talking about? Some scholars identify the cup as "the cup of God's
wrath" frequently mentioned by the Old Testament prophets (see
Isaiah 51:17; Jeremiah 25:15). However, a more basic connection
is the more immediate context of Passover, which Jesus had just
been celebrating.

I then turned to the Gospel of John. For John, the hour of Jesus's
passion, crucifixion, and death is also the hour of this greatest glory.
His abject humiliations constitute his exaltation; his apparent

defeat at the hands of his enemies is seen as his supreme triumph; his death is actually *the* event that brings life to the world.

So, the "it" that was finished was the Passover that Jesus had begun—but interrupted—in the Upper Room! Its completion was marked by Jesus drinking sour wine on Golgotha: the fourth cup. And Jesus calls us, as his disciples, to not only partake of the cup of blessing (the third cup) which we share in the Eucharist, but also of this fourth cup by dying for him (see Mark 10:38). Only then is the paschal mystery truly fulfilled in us.

+ Do I get in the way of what God desires to accomplish in and through me? How can my dying to self bring life to others?

Lord Jesus, the meaning and truth of your passion, crucifixion, and death can only be truly understood through the enlightenment of the Holy Spirit. I feel like I'm only beginning to contemplate this mystery, which you desire to be fulfilled in me.

HOLY THURSDAY

The Bread of Life

"Truly, truly, I say to you, unless you eat the flesh of the
Son of man and drink his blood, you have no life in you;
he who eats my flesh and drinks my blood has eternal
life, and I will raise him up at the last day."
—John 6:53–54

Jesus's discourse on the bread of life in John 6 sheds considerable light on the inseparable union between his Passover sacrifice in the Eucharist and on Calvary. John shows how Jesus miraculously provided bread for five thousand after he had "given thanks," evoking Eucharistic imagery. Jesus then identified himself as the "true bread from heaven" (v. 32) and the "bread of life" (v. 35), drawing a parallel with Moses, through whom God supernaturally fed manna to the Israelites while forming a covenant with them after the first Passover (see Exodus 16:4ff.). John thus prepares his readers to recognize how Jesus would form the New Covenant by means of his own Eucharistic sacrifice as high priest and paschal victim. In John 6:53–56, Jesus uses the strongest possible language to convey the truth of his real presence in the Eucharist as our paschal lamb. He makes it clear that his sacrificial death, begun in the Upper Room and finished on Golgotha, was the full end of his

Passover sacrifice. Since the main purpose is to restore communion, we too have to eat the Lamb. This is why Jesus instituted the Eucharist.

Paul shared a similar view of the matter, which he wrote to the Corinthians: "Christ, our paschal lamb, has been sacrificed" (1 Corinthians 5:7). He goes on to say in the very next verse, "Let us, therefore, celebrate the festival, not with the old leaven…but with the unleavened bread of sincerity and truth." In other words, Paul understood that something more remains for us to do. We must feast upon Jesus, the Bread of Life and our Passover Lamb.

+ As Lent draws to a close, what have I learned about my faith? Am I closer to Christ than when Lent began?

Lord Jesus, you are truly present in the Eucharist. Through it, we are united to you, in your flesh and blood, and part of the supernatural family of the New Adam. Thank you, Lord!

GOOD FRIDAY

A Once-for-All, Never-Ending Sacrifice

"He entered once for all into the Holy Place, taking not
the blood of goats and calves but his own blood, thus
securing an eternal redemption."

—Hebrews 9:12

The main theme of Hebrews is the priesthood of Jesus, particularly as it relates to his "once for all" sacrifice (see Hebrews 7:27; 9:12, 26; 10:10). Unlike the Jewish priests in the Old Covenant, Jesus doesn't make daily offerings of distinct sacrificial victims. On the other hand, as our High Priest, Jesus must have something to offer as a sacrifice on our behalf (see Hebrews 8:3). Contrary to Jesus's "once for all" sacrifice being exclusively past, this clearly implies that Jesus's sacrifice, precisely because of its "once for all" character, has become the one perfect offering that he continually presents in heaven. In other words, it's never-ending. That's why the Church calls it a "perpetual" sacrifice. As one of my teachers put it, "How can you repeat that which never ends?"

Jesus is no longer bleeding, suffering, or dying (see Hebrews 9:25–26). Rather, he is enthroned in heaven with his resurrected body and with our glorified humanity, which he as our older brother, High Priest, and King offers to the Father (see Hebrews

7:1–3). It is precisely in this manner that the Father beholds this perfect and perpetual offering in the living body of his Son.

The "once for all" character of Jesus's sacrifice points to the perfection and perpetuity of his self-offering. It can be represented upon our altars in the Eucharist, by the power of the Holy Spirit, so that "through him [we] continually offer up a sacrifice of praise to God" (Hebrews 13:15).

+ As a follower of Jesus, what qualities do I need to embrace? How can I make sure that I stay close to him, not forsaking my faith when I am discouraged?

Lord Jesus, you are priest, prophet, and king. You are the Messiah, the Son of God and the Lamb of God. You are all these things and more to fulfill all the promises made by the Father. Let me continually praise you for your sacrifice!

The Gospel of the New Covenant

"Jesus and the people he makes holy all belong to the
same family. That is why he's not ashamed to call them
his brothers and sisters."

—Hebrews 2:11

On this Holy Saturday, it seems appropriate to sum up the Gospel
of the New Covenant. It starts with the good news of creation:
God is more than the wise Creator; he is also our loving Father.
He established a covenant with us from the beginning, a sacred
family bond and a loving communion of trust and obedience—a
covenant that we have broken.

More than broken laws, sin results in broken lives, broken
homes, and broken hearts. The Father punishes sin with death,
because sin kills the life of God within us.

Sin's infection is deep and deadly, the solution came when Jesus
took on our weak and mortally wounded nature, not only to heal
and perfect us, but to elevate us to share in his own life of divine
sonship and make us one with his Father. Jesus seals the New
Covenant with us through his self-offering, first by instituting the
Eucharist, and then by dying for us on Calvary.

The Holy Spirit comes to us through the sacraments in a
powerful way, and the Eucharist is the greatest one of all. The

Catholic Church is God's worldwide family, established by Jesus through the Holy Spirit. We are to love the Church as our Mother, revere it as Christ's bride, and obey its teachings. And Jesus doesn't stop there—he gives us his mother, Mary, to be our own spiritual mother.

As God's children, we are earthly pilgrims heading home to heaven. Heaven is our true homeland, and death a true homecoming!

+ How close do I feel to Mary? Do I see her as *my* Mother?

Heavenly Father, from the very beginning you planned for us to be obedient, happy children here on earth, and together with you in heaven someday. No matter how many obstacles our willfulness and disobedience put in your path, you continue to show mercy and provide a new way for us to journey back to you, making us alive in Christ.

Easter Week

| HERE COMES THE BRIDE |

When people say *Church*, what generally comes to mind? Structure, institution, hierarchy, rules, buildings, St. Peter's Basilica, the pope? All this is true, but there's more to it.

In the book of Revelation, John describes a vision of the Church as the New Jerusalem and the Bride of Christ, beautiful and pure. Yet this vision of the Church does not always fit with the experience many people have: scandal, hypocrisy, bland liturgies, false teaching.

In this glorious Easter Week, we'll consider how Christ views the Church. This should help us to see ourselves—through the eyes of faith—as Christ sees us, even if we're all not yet canonizable saints.

EASTER SUNDAY

The Liturgy of Creation

"Thus it is written, that the Christ should suffer and on
the third day rise from the dead, and that repentance and
forgiveness of sins should be preached
in his name to all nations."

—Luke 24:46

The purpose of the New Covenant was not to abolish the earthly manifestations of the Old but to fulfill and expand them to their uttermost. Christ does this by rising from the dead and establishing the New Jerusalem—one worldwide family of God, the Catholic Church. As the Father's final and definitive Word, Jesus did it all. But he's still doing it, even now—through us, his Church—to fulfill his Father's promises.

In the book of Revelation, John describes the liturgy of creation (see chapter 4). Liturgy is worship of God by his creatures—a worship that is corporate, public, physical, orderly, and glorious. All the earth is God's temple; everything in it joins to worship the Creator, praising God in the liturgy of the cosmic temple.

That all creation finds a place in the liturgy of the cosmic temple is evident in various sacred symbols. The act of creation (see Genesis 1) established the liturgical rhythm of the Old Covenant.

God created the world in six days and rested on the seventh. God stamped this liturgical rhythm into both space and time, creating signs and seasons. "Seasons" are more than just spring, summer, winter, and fall; they refer to the festivals of covenant renewal.

The very being of creation worships God. Psalm 148 calls all levels of creation to praise the Lord: the heavens, the angelic hosts, the lights of the firmament, the earth, the sea, the mountains, the trees, the creatures, the elements. "Let them praise the name of the Lord! For he commanded and they were created" (Psalm 148:5).

+ During this Easter season, what is a simple way that I can add my praise to that of creation?

On this Easter Sunday, my heart is full of joy, O Lord! You have risen from the dead and you have ushered in a new creation. Praise the name of the Lord!

EASTER MONDAY

Faith in Invisible Realities

"By faith we understand the that world was created by
the word of God, so that what is seen was made out of
things which do not appear."

—Hebrews 11:3

An innumerable host of angels performs countless tasks in the ordering of creation. The angels are the instrumentalists; the things of creation are their instruments. Their service is the hymn of "Holy, Holy, Holy" before the throne of God, a command performance for the King and Creator and Author of the score.

At his creation, man participated in the symphony, but original sin produced discord. The union of divinity with humanity in the person of Jesus Christ reunited the physical and spiritual not just in man but in all creation. The drama of human salvation introduced the redemption of the entire world. The Incarnation reharmonized the symphony of creation.

The world was created to be a sacrament. In other words, everything on earth was made to point to human realities. Science has stripped reality down to a barren rationalism. In so doing it has blurred reality; faith corrects our vision so that we can see the splendor and mystery—and romance—that is reality.

+ What invisible realities do I see with my eyes of faith today?

Dear Lord, throughout the world you have placed signs that symbolize invisible realities, signs that point to you. Help me especially to recognize the realities behind the richness of the liturgy, all pointing to divine worship.

TUESDAY | EASTER WEEK

With Our Whole Being

"Worthy are you, our Lord and God, to receive glory and
honor and power, for you created all things, and by your
will they existed and were created."
—Revelation 4:11

God united divinity and humanity in the person of Christ not
to free us from our bodies but to redeem them and all creation.
God made us with souls and bodies, and he wants us to worship
him with our whole being. Bowing and kneeling, robes, thrones
and crowns, incense, candles, and bells aren't just nice extras. They
belong in our worship.

In Revelation 4, John describes the liturgy of creation, where the
living creatures and elders worship and glorify God who created
them (see verse 11). In Revelation 5, the liturgy of redemption,
they worship and glorify the Lamb whose blood redeemed them
(see verse 9). This is a unified liturgy with two distinct parts: One
celebrates God for making us, while the other celebrates Christ
for saving us.

The Lamb's sacrifice fashioned for God a kingdom of priests to
reign on earth. As royal priests, we offer ourselves, in union with
our High Priest and Lamb, as he offers himself to the Father on

our behalf. Our participation in the Eucharist gives us the power to plod along and overcome. History is controlled from the throne of the Lamb, but through the Church's liturgical worship, all of us can share in Christ's reign.

+ How can I express my devotion to you—not only with my mind, heart, and voice but also with my body?

Lord, you have made us to worship you with body, soul, and spirit. I can praise you by kneeling, by singing, by silent prayer, and by using holy water and incense. Thank you that I can worship you with my whole being!

WEDNESDAY | EASTER WEEK

A Lamb Who Was Slain—A Lion Who Reigns

"'To him who sits upon the throne and to the Lamb be
blessing and honor and glory and might for ever and
ever!' And the four living creatures said, 'Amen!' and the
elders fell down and worshiped."
—Revelation 5:13–14

In our liturgical worship, we approach Christ, the Lion who
reigns, the Lamb who was slain. The Mass ushers us into the presence of the Father and the Lamb, and into worship with the four
living creatures, the elders, the saints, and the myriad of angels.
Although we cannot see them, we share the dignity and privilege
of worshiping with them.

Our earthly worship environment should help us to see what
we can't see. It should strive to imitate its heavenly counterpart,
which we glimpse through Revelation. Too often our liturgical art,
music, and architecture bow to utility and economy, when they
should bow to the transcendent. John's vision inspires us to rethink
the ways we design our churches. The visible should be a vehicle
for the invisible, giving our sense a taste of the glorious mystery
in which we partake, filling our beings with reverence and awe,
lifting our minds and hearts to heaven.

In Revelation we discover our vital role as royal priests, as we affect the course of history and the destiny of nations through our worship. God's sovereignty extends to the whole world, but he exercises his rule—and executes his saving plan—in conjunction with the Church at prayer. We are part of a grand battle plan.

+ Do I realize that participating in the liturgy literally affects the course of history? What does this awareness do to the value I place on being part of the Church?

Dear God, your heavenly liturgy is important, and participating in it is important too. You avenge our suffering, protect and deliver us, and influence the course of history, all in response to the liturgy. May I never take it for granted!

The Beautiful Bride of Christ

"This is a great mystery…I mean in reference
to Christ and the Church."
—Ephesians 5:32

In the opening verses of John's final vision, the Church is described in two ways: as the holy city, the new Jerusalem; and as the beautiful Bride of Christ (see Revelation 21:1–2). Paul tells us, "Now you are the body of Christ and individually members of it" (1 Corinthians 12:27). As members of the Church, we are members of Christ's body through participation in the Eucharist (see 1 Corinthians 10:17).

When God first made man, he formed the marital covenant. He caused Eve to come forth from Adam's side. When he saw her, Adam proclaimed her "bone of my bones and flesh of my flesh" (Genesis 2:23). At the beginning of time, God drew an image of what things would be like at the end. Adam and Eve became natural, physical, earthly signs of a supernatural, spiritual, heavenly reality: Jesus Christ and his Church. The Church is Christ's body just as Eve was Adam's.

From Adam's side came forth one who was both body and bride: Eve, formed from his body, was bone of his bone, flesh of his flesh. Joined to him in marriage, she became one body with him.

Similarly, from the side of Christ pierced with a lance came the Church. Just as Eve came from Adam and was united with him as one body, so the Church comes from Christ and is united to him as one body. The Church is Christ's Body, and as such is his Bride. The Church is Christ's Bride, and as such is his Body.

+ As the bride of Christ, how can I deepen my intimacy with him?

Lord Jesus, it is a privilege to be a part of your Church. To know that, as the Church, we are your Bride is a remarkable vision. Thank you, Lord.

Union With God

"Husbands, love your wives, as Christ loved the Church
and gave himself up for her, that he might sanctify her,
having cleansed her by the washing of the water with the
word, that he might present the Church to himself in
splendor, without spot or wrinkle or any such thing, that
she might be holy and without blemish."

—Ephesians 5:25–27

The marital imagery of Christ's love for his Church becomes a powerful symbol for the sacrament of marriage. Just as God's Fatherhood is the perfect reality that human fatherhood portrayed, though imperfectly, so the marriage of Christ and the Church is the perfect reality portrayed by human marriage. Our vision for marital love and sexual intimacy should reflect this reality.

Western society has made an idol out of sex. Sex dominates our entertainment, it sells our cars, it controls the way we think of ourselves. Our society is driven by sex; it lives for sex. Our longing for sexual intimacy is among our deepest desires and strongest passions. God has placed in us these natural desires, which reflect supernatural desires fulfilled only in him.

For example, we hunger for food. We eat food; we are filled. This images a spiritual longing within us, satisfied only when God fills us with himself. We long for beauty. We discover it in the things around us, but only when God's beauty ravishes us do we find peace. We desire intimacy and sexual union, and we find it in other persons. But that desire points to a deeper desire, which only union with God can meet. Union with God proves to be deep intimacy and unimaginable ecstasy, infinite fulfillment of the desire to love and be loved.

This is a truth that only the mystic can really understand; but then, mystics are lovers. And God wants all of us to be lovers.

+ Do I view marriage in a sacramental way? What can I do to affirm the value of marriage in today's society?

Lord Jesus, let me always remember that marriage and family life are meant to be a sign of your intimate union with your bride, the Church. Marriage is a precious sign of the intense love you have for each of us.

SATURDAY OF EASTER WEEK

The Dwelling of God

"Behold, the dwelling of God is with men.
He will dwell with them, and they shall be his people,
nd God himself will be with them."
—Revelation 21:3

In the Old Testament God took Israel as his bride. When she played the harlot, the Lord cast her off (see Ezekiel 16:59; Hosea 1—3). But he did not abandon her forever. He promised to remember his covenant and establish with her an everlasting covenant.

What God did in the Old Testament through Israel, God is continuing in the New Testament Church today. He is fathering his family, restoring the human race to his household. And while the kingdom of God can never fully be realized on earth, it does find partial (yet real) fulfillment in us on this side of heaven. We experience the fulfillment of the New Covenant now—through the Church.

When we become members of the Church, we become citizens of the heavenly Jerusalem. Through the liturgy, through the sacraments, in the prayers and works of the people of God, we participate in heavenly life.

We don't experience this heavenly life with our earthly senses, but it is real—more real than the physical world. When the world ends, the Church will continue triumphant in heaven, and we will see and experience God's life fully, completely, ecstatically, and eternally.

+ How real is heaven to me? Do I see it as someplace far away and removed from life here on earth, or is heaven more real than the physical reality around me?

Dear God, you promise to make all things new. Help me to see with the eyes of faith, so that I can discern eternity in the midst of this earthly realm and look forward with great anticipation to what lies ahead.

DIVINE MERCY SUNDAY

Becoming Saints

"For we have not a high priest who is unable to
sympathize with our weaknesses, but one who in every
respect has been tempted as we are, yet without sinning.
Let us then with confidence draw near to the throne of
grace, that we may receive mercy and find grace to help
in time of need."

—Hebrews 4:15–16

It may seem that the Church John envisions in Revelation is a far
cry from the Church we have experienced. We see scandal and
hypocrisy, bland liturgies, false teaching, broken families, sin and
sinners everywhere.

We have to remember: "We walk by faith, not by sight"
(2 Corinthians 5:7). By faith we understand that the Church's
essential identity is heavenly. We can't judge her by our earthly
experience. She is only fully herself in heaven.

Here on earth the Church is a field full of both wheat and weeds
(see Matthew 13:24–30, 36–43). But she is really and truly the
heavenly kingdom here on earth. Through Scripture we must train
ourselves to attain a sacramental vision of the Church. When you
allow scandal to make you leave the Church, you are not only

depriving yourself of spiritual food (the sacraments), you are spurning Christ's Bride.

Sinners are in the Church, but they do not embody the Church. For them the Church is a hospital for healing, so they can be made into saints. The sacraments, the liturgy, and especially the saints embody the Church's true essence.

The real crisis in the Church today is a crisis of saints. But we can trust our Father to handle this; we can trust him to keep his promises to us. "He who began a good work in you will bring it to completion at the day of Jesus Christ" (Philippians 1:6). So with Blessed John Paul II, I urge you, "Make yourselves saints, and do so quickly!"

+ Do I trust God to make me a saint—and quickly?

Lord Jesus, thank you for the Feast of Divine Mercy! Your mercy is a shelter for all souls, especially for sinners. I want to experience the depths of your grace and mercy—it's the only way for someone like me to become a saint.

About the Author

Dr. Scott Hahn, professor of theology and Scripture at Franciscan University of Steubenville since 1990, is a popular speaker, teacher, and author. His talks and writings have been effective in helping thousands of Protestants and fallen-away Catholics to re-embrace the Catholic faith. He is the founder and director of the Saint Paul Center for Biblical Theology, and in 2005 he was appointed as the Pope Benedict XVI Chair of Biblical Theology and Liturgical Proclamation at St. Vincent Seminary in Latrobe, Pennsylvania. Scott Hahn and his wife, Kimberly, have six children and five grandchildren.